LIFE IN
The 1970s

Carol Harris

The Home

The 1970s home was a combination of the very modern and the traditional. Walls were often decorated in wood panelling and wallpaper covered a wide range of styles, from woodchip to bold geometric patterns. Growing concern over the environment was reflected in housing through more energy-efficient homes and in decor, with the trend for a home-crafted look such as pine-stripped furniture and heavy pottery. Furniture could be modern, typically by G-Plan or Schreiber, or, for the more traditional 'country cottage' styling, by Ercol (made of solid elm and beech). Whatever the style of furnishings and furniture, the 'lava lamp' was a common feature.

Growing consumer power was reflected everywhere in the home. Two-thirds of the population owned washing machines. Most other people relied on local launderettes for washing and drying clothes.

Microwave ovens became cheaper and more commonplace over the decade, but people had to be taught how to use them at local classes or through magazine articles. Similarly, the colour television went from being a luxury to a standard item in the main living room. In 1970 over 90 per cent of homes had sets, but only 273,000 had colour televisions, and 15 million watched in black and white; by 1979 more than twice as many

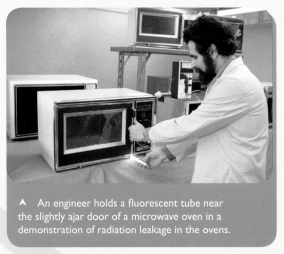

∧ An engineer holds a fluorescent tube near the slightly ajar door of a microwave oven in a demonstration of radiation leakage in the ovens.

homes (over 12 million) had a colour television as had a black and white one. Portable sets were available but most homes had only one television as they were still expensive compared to today.

Telephones had previously been owned only by the better-off, but during the 1970s many homes acquired one. The fashionable telephone was the sleek 'Trimphone' which bleeped rather than rang; neither this nor the more traditional models were cordless. There was usually only one phone in a house, shared by all the family, and usually located in the hall.

◄ A modern bathroom painted in orange is presented at the German Furniture Fair in 1973 in Cologne.

▲ The Postmaster General, Anthony Wedgwood Benn, demonstrates the new Trimphone.

Some homes still lacked even basic facilities. The 1971 General Household Survey reported that 10 per cent of people had an outside toilet in their homes and 1 per cent had no toilet at all. The same survey showed that 9 per cent did not have a bath; showering was seen mainly as an additional way of washing, not an alternative to bathing. Most showers were installed over baths in family homes.

Tower blocks of flats had seemed to be the way to provide low-cost, high-density homes for people, but by the 1970s tower blocks were increasingly associated with street crime, vandalism and urban decay.

More people bought their own homes in the 1970s, but building societies would lend money for mortgages only if you had a substantial deposit and what the lender decided was sufficient regular income. As wages rose, so too did house prices. In 1970 the average house cost £4,975; by 1979 it had risen to £19,925. Some council tenants bought through 'right to buy' schemes, under which they could purchase the homes they lived in at a heavy discount. In 1970, 7,000 council homes were sold to tenants; by 1972 this had increased to nearly 46,000.

Working Lives

Over the decade unemployment leapt from 2.7 per cent to 7.4 per cent and inflation soared, reaching a huge 27 per cent in 1975. Governments tried to control the UK economy through limits on wage rises. Negotiations between the Government, TUC (the umbrella body for all trade unions) and the CBI (the equivalent body for employers) throughout the decade resulted in various agreements to control prices and pay rises.

Most people worked 35 to 40 hours a week, many of them in manufacturing. However, these industries were in decline and job losses mounted as other countries began to produce cheaper goods. Manufacturers were reluctant to modernise and so too were unions representing the workers in these declining industries. Even so, by 1978 nearly 29 per cent of the population still worked in factories.

Trade union membership, which had grown steadily since the Second World War, reached its peak in the 1970s. Over 13 million unskilled, skilled and professional workers were members.

A major change was the increase in the number of women entering the workforce. The Equal Pay Act of 1970 made it illegal to pay different rates of pay to men and women doing broadly similar jobs – although it did not apply to Northern Ireland. Employers were given five years to make the necessary changes but many used the time to re-grade jobs and titles to perpetuate lower pay for women. Women joined trade unions in increasing numbers as legislation on equality did not bring the expected changes in pay and opportunities.

Many women went into office work, increasingly based around micro-computers and word processors. These were the forerunners of today's laptops and replaced the enormous

▲ A Meriden worker fits an engine to a Bonneville motorcycle in the former Norton Villiers Triumph factory, which became a workers' co-operative backed by £5 million from the Government, 1975.

▲ Members of the public, anticipating power cuts, patiently queue outside a Fleet Street shop to purchase candles.

▲ Public service workers take part in a mass march to the Houses of Parliament as part of a 'day of action' against Government pay policy, January 1979.

mainframe computers which had been a feature of office work in the 1960s.

Britain gained a reputation for poor labour relations, especially among public sector workers and in nationalised industries such as car manufacturing, steel and transport. Miners in the mainly nationalised coal industry were among the lowest paid in the country and there was widespread public sympathy when they went on strike for a large pay increase in January 1972. Coal supplies dwindled and the Government introduced a three-day working week to preserve stocks essential for Britain's coal-fired electricity-generating stations. A second strike was called in 1974, when the Government once again declared a state of emergency and brought back the three-day week.

Despite the headlines, most unions and employers worked effectively together, and pay and conditions improved. However, pay rises for people working in the public sector were kept deliberately lower than price rises as an anti-inflation measure. As a result, strikes were widespread in the public sector; strikers included firemen, cleaners and junior doctors. As the decade came to an end, council workers went on strike in what became known as the Winter of Discontent; rubbish went uncollected and picket lines turned people away at hospitals and graveyards.

Union membership was declining by the end of the decade and in the election campaign of 1979, Margaret Thatcher called for curbs on workers' rights and limits on trade union power.

◄ Conservative leader Margaret Thatcher in a thoughtful mood as she hosts a party press conference in London, 1979.

Another major change was the introduction of decimal currency. The new, simpler system of 100 pennies to the pound replaced the system in which 12 pennies made a shilling and 20 shillings one pound. Television programmes and public information campaigns explained the new currency and the move was viewed favourably by most.

Continuing the trend from the 60s, self-service supermarkets took over the high street and shopping centres (based on American shopping malls) opened up. The first out-of-town shopping centre opened in Brent Cross in 1976. It had 86 shops and parking for 5,000 cars.

Small, local shops selling specific items could not compete with supermarkets where people could do all their shopping in one place. Many small grocers closed down but the Co-op thrived

▲ The new hand-held calculator in the 1970s.

and competed with other supermarkets such as Tesco, Safeway and Fine Fare. Sainsbury's and British Home Stores combined to open Savacentre, selling goods from both shops under the slogan 'The store with more for less'.

Fridges and freezers became commonplace so people did not need to buy food on a daily basis. Shopping became a leisure activity for some but for others, especially working women who were almost always responsible for food shopping, it had to be fitted in on Saturdays.

The tradition of half-day closing, and of closing at lunchtime, died out over the course of the decade, but at the start, most shops were only open during the week and on Saturdays from 9 a.m. to 5.30 p.m. Trading on Sundays was banned.

A plethora of new and affordable items arrived on the high street for the first time. These included electrical goods such as the pocket calculator (1971), microwave oven (1974), the video recorder (1978) and the Sony Walkman (1979).

Frozen and dehydrated foods became enormously popular, part of a trend for 'convenience' foods. Brand leaders included Birds

◀ Lord Fiske, Chairman of the Decimal Currency Board, shows a poster which is to be displayed in order to explain the new decimal currency, 1970.

Eye beef burgers, Smash instant mashed potato, Chef dried soup, and Vesta ready meals – these presented very British versions of the foods people were buying at takeaways, such as chicken curry, paella and chow mein.

In 1972 McDougall's flour introduced the first ready-mixed shortcrust and flaky pastry. But the reaction against processed foods was beginning to take hold. Brown bread sales increased throughout the decade as people rejected heavily processed white pre-sliced loaves.

One new item – best used with sliced bread – was another 1970s invention: the sandwich toaster, developed in Australia in 1974.

Mail order shopping from catalogues such as Freeman's, Trafford or Grattan expanded. People selected items from these catalogues, which were filled with glossy colour photographs. The goods were often more expensive than in the shops but could be paid for in instalments.

Some stores gave shoppers stamps with their purchases. One leader in this approach was the Co-op, which issued its 'divi' to members in this way. Tesco shoppers received Green Shield stamps which could be exchanged for goods from catalogues at Green Shield's own shops (called Gift Houses). In 1973 Green Shield was rebranded as Argos and customers were also able to pay in cash.

Relationships

▲ A typical nuclear family playing in the park in 1975.

People's attitudes towards relationships had changed rapidly during and since the Second World War. These shifts were reflected in legislation passed in the 1960s which meant the 1970s displayed a far more liberal official attitude to how people could live together. However, the state still treated one type of relationship – for example, a nuclear family headed by two white, heterosexual parents – more favourably than others.

Few couples lived together without being married. In 1971 the average household size in Great Britain was 2.9 people, with one-person households accounting for just 18 per cent of the total – much lower than it is today. Women

▲ US women marching in protest in 1977.

◄ A gay demonstration at the Old Bailey in London, 1977.

husbands had little support. Campaigners for women's rights such as Erin Pizzey, who set up Chiswick Women's Aid, argued for refuges, where battered wives could stay with their children. In 1976 laws to protect female victims of domestic violence were introduced.

Race relations were a hotly debated topic. Racial discrimination was outlawed in 1976, although the legislation did not apply to Northern Ireland. It became illegal to discriminate on the grounds of racial origin in areas such as employment, training, housing, education and in providing goods, facilities and services. The Commission for Racial Equality was established to combat discrimination.

Gay rights were another important focus at this time. In 1967 homosexual acts between men in private were legalised in England and Wales (lesbian sex was never outlawed in this way). During the 1970s, civil rights groups called for further reform and campaigned against discrimination at work and in the home. Issues included making the age of consent equal to that for heterosexual relationships, not sacking someone for being gay, and allowing lesbians to have access to and custody of children following divorce.

had children at a younger age – in 1971, 47 per cent of babies born in England and Wales had mothers under 25; by 2008 this had dropped to 25 per cent.

There was a huge increase in the number of divorces following the 1969 Divorce Reform Act, which had made marital breakdown the main reason for divorce. Previously, the law had said that one partner had to be at fault, and that person would have few rights. Now, the courts would grant a divorce after a couple had lived apart for a specified time.

Traditionalists argued that this more liberal approach was causing the break-up of families. Others said that in the traditional family, the problem was that the only person with any power was the husband. Radical psychologists argued that in a typical nuclear family, personal freedom and individuality were stifled, power was unevenly shared, and intimacy was a byword for fear, tension and conflict.

Public debate over violence against women was started by campaigns to highlight domestic abuse, most of which was by husbands against wives. Police were often reluctant to intervene in 'domestics' and women choosing to leave violent

▲ The Rock Against Racism concert in 1978.

Childhood

Schooling, especially for older children, faced massive change in 1973, when the school-leaving age was increased from 15 to 16. A new school-leaving exam, the Certificate of Secondary Education (CSE), was added to the existing O levels taken at 16 and A levels at 18.

New subjects on the curriculum included British Constitution and Business Studies. Many schools ended gender restrictions so that, for example, girls could now study metalwork and woodwork, and boys could study home economics (mainly cookery) and business studies.

Numbers going on to university increased to 14 per cent, the highest number ever at that point.

For younger children, there were too few nurseries for all to have a place so many did not start education until they went to school. Demand increased as more and more mothers with young children went out to work, but by 1980 both nursery education and day nursery care were increasingly confined to children in deprived areas.

Children spent much of their free time out of doors. Toy marketing was often gender specific – boys would ride around on the new Chopper bicycles by Raleigh. A Chopper was good for doing wheelies (riding on the back wheel only) and was designed to look like a motorcycle when propped up on its stand. For girls there were dolls such as Cabbage Patch Kids, created in the USA in 1978.

Such stereotyping was increasingly challenged throughout the 1970s and as the decade progressed toys became more gender neutral,

▲ Children on bikes in Edenbridge, Kent, 1975.

> Children skateboarding in the mid-1970s.

◀ A Rubik's cube.

such as space hoppers and skateboards. There were crazes such as the Rubik's Cube and Clackers. Clackers were plastic balls on a string which were swung at increasing speed to make a loud 'clacking' sound, satisfyingly annoying to grown-ups.

Millions watched children's television. Innovative programmes included *Multi-Coloured Swap Shop*, which was broadcast on Saturday mornings on BBC1 and pioneered the phone-in. At the same time on ITV was *Tiswas*, a similar but more anarchic children's programme in which buckets of water were thrown over everyone.

Other popular toys included the stunt kite (invented in 1976) and action figures – those linked to the film *Star Wars* became bestsellers.

Pocket money could be spent on ice creams; Wall's and Lyons Maid were at their most commercially successful, with new lollies such as 'Haunted House' and some linked to television programmes like *Space 1999*. Chocolate and sweets aimed at children included Curly Wurlys (launched in 1970).

Concern in the early 1970s about the need for children to be parented in permanent families led to the Children Act 1975, which extended the rights of both children, foster parents, adoptive parents and local authorities, and reduced those of the natural parent. The following year the Adoption Act allowed anyone who had been adopted the right to see their original birth certificate and be given information about their biological parents.

Following the outcry at the death in 1973 of 7-year-old Maria Colwell, care for the most vulnerable children was reviewed and major changes proposed, but many reforms were ineffectually implemented.

Science & Technology

Video games, personal computers and pocket calculators all had their origins in the 1970s. The first home computing machines arrived at this time – popular models were from Commodore and Apple, and the 'BBC micro', originally developed for the BBC, was used widely.

The popularity of the tennis game 'Pong' was a forerunner of today's billion-pound home videogames industry, even though it was two-dimensional, in black and white (or livid green), and for a maximum of two players. Space Invaders, available on a coin-operated machine, was invented in Japan in 1978. Usually located in pubs, it was the first colour game most people encountered.

Television viewing underwent a major change with the arrival of home video recorders. A battle between the two main rival systems, VHS and Betamax, resulted in a win for the VHS format. The deciding factor was not which one of them offered the better quality picture (generally agreed to be Betamax), but which system could offer the widest range of pre-recorded films, which people rented from the new video hire shops. Tape was also taking over from vinyl for music in the form of the compact cassette, which led in 1979 to the Walkman.

The US space programme, which had achieved the first landing on the moon in 1968, continued with four more moon landings in 1971–72. Their Russian rivals concentrated instead on developing space stations, launching the first, the Salyut 1 laboratory, in April 1970. On the second mission, the three-man crew successfully docked and entered the space station and stayed a record 22 days, but died on the return journey.

▲ Sony Corporation's very first Walkman, from 1979.

◄ The general manager of RCA Corporation consumer-electronics operations demonstrates a new video tape machine in 1977.

▲ The Saturn V rocket, topped by Skylab I, sits on the launch site at Kennedy Space Center in Cape Kennedy, 1973.

Other major technical advances came through discoveries in solid state physics, from which came lasers and integrated circuits. Digital displays, presenting more accurate and visible signs, became commonplace, first with the digital watch, most famously by Swatch, followed by the pocket calculator and even a wristwatch and calculator combined.

Excitement at these new technologies was tempered by growing concern about man's impact on the environment. One important issue at this time was whether energy produced by nuclear power could safely replace the polluting fossil-fuelled power stations.

The space race was effectively over by 1975, when the two superpowers instead began collaborating on the Joint Apollo-Soyuz Test Project (ASTP). American efforts resulted in the space station Skylab, and a shift in emphasis towards developing the 'shuttle' (reusable) spacecraft.

Space exploration advanced further than ever before with the Voyager programme. In 1977, two unmanned spaceships, Voyager 1 and 2, began their journeys to explore the outer reaches of the solar system. Space and cosmology were the focus of more theoretical science, too. The scientist Stephen Hawking led debates over black holes and the origins of the universe.

More immediate breakthroughs were made with the introduction of fibre optics, which would revolutionise the telecommunications and computing industries. These optical fibres were tubes of high-quality glass or plastic, each similar in diameter to a human hair, down which light could be transmitted.

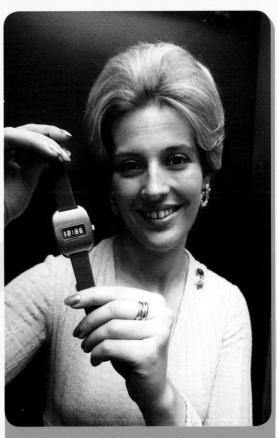

▲ The new liquid crystal watch featuring no movable parts and a digital readout, 1972.

Health

In 1970 about half the population smoked; life expectancy in the UK was just 69 years for a man and 75 years for a woman, mainly because of this habit. Getting people to give up was the public health issue of the decade.

People smoked everywhere: at home, in the workplace, and in restaurants, theatres and cinemas. This began to change, at first with designated smoke-free zones in public places, and later with total bans on smoking, representing a shift from smoking as the norm.

Nearly a quarter of pregnant women smoked; a new campaign tackled smoking in pregnancy, highlighting the dangers to the unborn child.

Tobacco companies countered these measures by targeting women (who did not smoke as much as men) and sponsoring sports events, so their logos were visible on television. In 1979

▲ Actress Glenda Jackson with a smile and a cigarette in London in 1974.

the tobacco industry helped to fund a new organisation, FOREST, which campaigned against the warnings by arguing that smoking was about personal freedom and choice.

The 1967 Abortion Act had made the termination of pregnancy generally available on the NHS, and deaths from illegal abortions continued to fall. Family planning clinics offered advice, health checks and prescriptions for all types of contraceptives. The contraceptive pill was now available on demand to all women over 16 in the UK.

Mental health was a controversial issue. Those affected wanted more say in their treatment and to have services available in their local

How can another woman make you pregnant?

Just by talking to you. And giving you bad advice. Too many women risk getting bad advice about contraception because they'd rather listen to friends than go to a clinic or a doctor. No wonder there are 120,000 unwanted babies born in Britain every year. No matter if you're young or old, married or single, you can get help and advice that is friendly, private, and above all, accurate, from your doctor or local family planning clinic. **The Health Education Council** ⊙

You can find your local clinic under 'Family Planning' in the telephone directory or Yellow Pages. Or write to, The Health Education Council, 78 New Oxford Street, London WC1A 1AH.

◄ Poster from the HEC family planning campaign which tells people how to prevent unwanted babies.

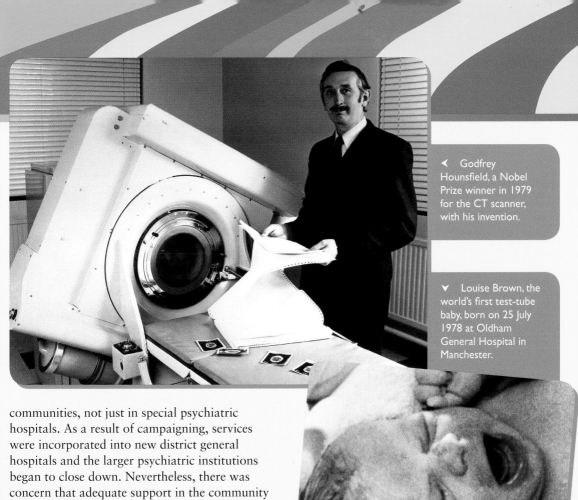

communities, not just in special psychiatric hospitals. As a result of campaigning, services were incorporated into new district general hospitals and the larger psychiatric institutions began to close down. Nevertheless, there was concern that adequate support in the community was not in place, and it became a major issue in coming decades.

Legislation to help disabled people live and work in the community rather than in residential care homes was introduced. These new laws meant that every disabled person was entitled to an assessment of their needs; however, crucially, the laws did not guarantee funding to meet the needs identified. Small allowances for those caring for older and disabled people were also introduced at this time, but close relatives and those not of working age – the majority of carers – were excluded.

Better coordination of services was the primary aim of reorganisations of the NHS and Local Government. In addition, new medical treatments and technologies were introduced, like CT scanners in 1972. With a CT scanner, the human body could be scanned in three dimensions, greatly improving diagnosis. In 1978 magnetic resonance imaging was unveiled, in the first whole body MRI scanner.

Also in 1978, British doctors developed *in vitro* fertilisation, fertilising an egg outside a woman's body before replacing it in the womb.

Transplant surgery was becoming more commonplace and donor registers were established. A kidney donor card was established in 1971, and the following year the National Organ Matching and Distribution Service was founded. As transplant surgery improved, this database was needed to ensure the best match between donated organs and waiting patients. In its first 11 months, 455 kidney transplants were carried out with matching achieved through the database.

Fashion

ashion in the early 1970s combined the modern with traditional and home-made styles. Discotheques were the places to wear satins, miniskirts and skin-tight clothing. Second-hand and recycled clothing, known as 'Oxfam chic', held its popularity throughout the decade, and the growing popularity of crafts such as crochet, knitting and beadwork was reflected in decorations and accessories.

The ethnic look made popular traditional styles from all over the world. Hippies popularised loose, flowing clothing from India and Nepal, and the home-sewn beading of Native Americans. High fashion drew from Japanese designers such as Kenzo and Kansai Yamamoto. They introduced the 'Big Look' of over-sized shirts and cowboy boots.

Fabrics could be patchwork or tie-dyed; Laura Ashley created an international brand featuring her floral, Victorian-style printed cottons, worn over layers of lace-edged petticoats. Biba also looked back to the style of another era. Founded by Barbara Hulanicki in the 1960s, Biba opened a department store in 1970 which recreated the glamour and sophistication of the 1930s and 1940s.

The unisex look took off, with denim jeans and dungarees, and tank tops in bright and contrasting colours. New brands of jeans such as Brutus and Wrangler appeared; brushed, washed, patched and coloured denim was the fabric of

▲ Moya Gillett and Lina Huby model paper minidresses in London, 1970, for Dispo '70, Britain's first exhibition and conference for disposable clothing. One is a simple style mini-kaftan and the other a psychedelic-patterned minidress.

◄ Dave Hill, the guitarist of the glam rock group Slade, in 1975.

minis, more so as the decade wore on. Kaftans were popular with women who favoured the ethnic look, but were less successful as unisex garments. Evening wear for women now included trousers and catsuits, though some traditional places banned them.

On the high street, Calvin Klein and Ralph Lauren became international names.

The cinema continued to influence: Katherine Ross summed up the floaty romantic style for women in the film *Butch Cassidy and the Sundance Kid*; the male craze for white suits was sparked by John Travolta in *Saturday Night Fever*. 'Blaxploitation' films such as *Shaft* created male trends for leather jackets and polo-neck jumpers.

Followers of glam rock, seen onstage in the costumes of David Bowie, Elton John and Roxy Music, wore outrageous outfits in metallic, velvet and satin. Then as the decade wore on, punk styles took off. Punk was initially a reaction to the commercialism of the fashion industry, and featured deliberately slashed clothing, home-styled tattoos and tops made from plastic bin liners. Paradoxically, its leading designer was Vivienne Westwood, who sold bondage trousers, leather, rubber and plastic clothing from a shop on the King's Road.

the decade. The overall shape emphasised legs and waists through high-waisted, flared trousers. These were known as 'bell-bottoms' or 'loons' – from 'balloon trousers' – and there was a revival of 'Oxford Bags', originally worn by men in the 1920s and now a popular unisex item.

In footwear, platform soles, often in contrasting colours, and stacked and wedge heels added height and lengthened legs. Among younger people hair was unisex too, with men and women opting for tight 'bubble' perms and the layered feather cut.

Women's fashions were romantic and nostalgic. Maxi (full-length) and midi (mid-calf) skirts and dresses were as popular as

Popular Culture

With just two television companies – BBC and ITV – broadcasting on three channels, television audiences for programmes were enormous. Tens of millions watched the most popular programmes. These included game shows such as Bruce Forsyth's *Generation Game* and *Sale of the Century*; comedy shows from Benny Hill and Morecambe and Wise; and soap operas such as *Coronation Street* and *Crossroads*.

Popular period dramas such as *Upstairs, Downstairs* started at this time. More 'serious' programmes included classics such as the BBC production of *I, Claudius* and series by contemporary writers like the controversial Andrea Newman, who wrote *A Bouquet of Barbed Wire*.

American programmes took up a substantial part of the television schedules, especially detective series like *Columbo* and *Kojak* which were shown at peak times. Equally popular were

▲ Presenter Bruce Forsyth.

the macho men of British dramas such as *The Sweeney* and *The Professionals*.

Significant changes were recommended in the Annan Report which affected the future of broadcasting; a major restructuring of television took place, Channel 4 was created and there was a substantial increase in the licence fee.

ITV was a network of regional stations; the various companies such as Anglia, Thames and Granada became extremely wealthy as they were funded by commercials. With a guaranteed audience of tens of millions at peak times, any products advertised would almost inevitably become brand leaders. The advertisements reflected contemporary values – women were

◄ Peter Falk as homicide detective Lieutenant Columbo, 1972.

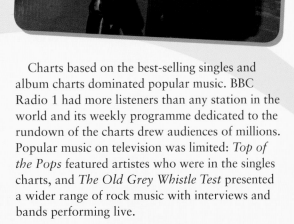

almost always the focus of ads for cooking and laundry in the home; ads for cars were aimed at men.

The massive increase in the number of colour televisions in the home led to a further decline in numbers going to the cinema. One way in which cinemas responded was by showing films which depicted scenes prohibited from television screens – usually relating to sex and violence – over which there were strict rules for television.

Films which became notorious for their violence and horror, such as *The Exorcist*, were major box-office draws, as were Bruce Lee's *Kung Fu* films and the *Dirty Harry* series. The *Emmanuelle* films did the same with sex, and even British-made Hammer films increasingly added sexual content to their horror films.

Disaster films with all-star casts such as *The Towering Inferno* and *The Poseidon Adventure* were enormously popular; westerns were out of fashion, but science fiction films, particularly *Star Wars* and *Star Trek: the Motion Picture*, broke box office records and presented the latest special effects.

Popular music included disco, with groups such as Boney M; pop, dominated by the Swedish group Abba; prog (progressive) rock, played by groups such as Yes and Pink Floyd, and from the mid-1970s, punk rock with groups like the Sex Pistols.

Charts based on the best-selling singles and album charts dominated popular music. BBC Radio 1 had more listeners than any station in the world and its weekly programme dedicated to the rundown of the charts drew audiences of millions. Popular music on television was limited: *Top of the Pops* featured artists who were in the singles charts, and *The Old Grey Whistle Test* presented a wider range of rock music with interviews and bands performing live.

Transport

Road was the preferred way of travelling at the beginning of the 1970s. The railways were in decline and people preferred to drive on the new motorways. These roads linked towns and cities in complex new road schemes designed to ease congestion. The early 70s saw the opening of two of the biggest interchanges, both of which were nicknamed 'Spaghetti Junction'. With 17 parallel lanes, the Worsley Braided Interchange on the M61 has more lanes than any road in the world.

However, concerns were growing about pollution and especially the emissions of petrol-fuelled cars and lorries, which deposited high levels of lead into the atmosphere. The oil crisis of 1973 added to this shift in attitudes. The enormous increase in the price of petrol affected all forms of transport. New models of car emphasised fuel efficiency.

By the mid-1970s, rules for planning new transport systems meant that local councils had to take into account factors such as impact on the environment and how accessible transport was to people on lower incomes. As a result, the number of planned road schemes reduced.

Car ownership increased significantly, however. At the beginning of the decade, 52 per cent of households in Britain had regular use of a car; there were 11.2 million private and light goods vehicles, and 2.3 million other vehicles (mostly lorries) licensed. By 1980, this had increased to 16 million and 3 million respectively.

Car production was a major industry. One of the most popular and iconic models of the decade was the Ford Capri, which was produced at the Halewood plant in Liverpool. Eleven years after the Capri was launched it was still among the top ten best-selling cars in Britain.

Train travel declined significantly. The UK train system was a national network under British Rail, but it suffered from a reputation for poor service, dirty facilities and rolling stock,

◀ Spaghetti Junction at Gravelly Hill in Birmingham, 1972.

▲ British Rail's new High Speed Train.

◄ Racing driver Jackie Stewart with the new Ford Capri RS 3100, 1973.

and appalling industrial relations. The number of rail users – passengers and freight – fell, only increasing as the company began to invest in High Speed Trains.

For most people, public transport meant buses which, like railways, were publicly owned in a nationally coordinated network. Here the major visible change was the end of the bus conductor on all but the busiest routes. Now one person drove the bus and collected the fares. It took longer but meant that costs could be significantly reduced.

Package tours combining cheap flights and accommodation offered many people the chance to fly overseas for their holidays. In 1971 people from the UK made 6.7 million holiday trips abroad. Destinations such as Spain, Majorca and Portugal had a major advantage over UK-based destinations because the weather was notably better. In the 1970s, Crete and the

Algarve became the favoured destinations, but the reputation and popularity of such package holidays declined significantly when in 1974 Court Line, the second largest tour operator, collapsed and 50,000 holidaymakers were stranded overseas; up to 100,000 more lost their deposits.

▲ Pan American Airways' massive new Boeing 747 jumbo jet after its first ever landing at Heathrow Airport in 1970.

Famous Faces

Celebrities had been known for many years collectively as the jet set – because of the way they travelled from one fashionable centre to another – or the Beautiful People. In the 1970s the supersonic Anglo-French Concorde airliner was the glamorous way to travel and its scheduled flights were usually met by press photographers who snapped the more famous passengers.

The term 'supermodel' was widely used. This referred to women so famous as models that they could command extraordinarily high fees. At first the fashionable style was typified by 1960s British model Jean Shrimpton – tall, thin, with straight hair and long legs. But by the mid-1970s, the typical supermodel was Margaux Hemingway, a curvy and tanned Californian.

Throughout the early 1970s, the Miss World international beauty contest was making its winners famous. The 1970 event, however, provoked angry reactions, first by women objecting to the idea of a competition that assessed women purely on looks, and then, even more controversially, because apartheid South Africa was allowed to participate,

entering a white contestant and a 'coloured' contestant, who in the event came second.

Northern Ireland's George Best had talent, money and good looks, and he became the first celebrity footballer – typically photographed out at night with a host of young women. The gossip columnists also followed the Beatles as they documented their solo careers, their feuds, and their changing partners and wives. Equally famous were The Rolling Stones, whose world tours were disrupted by arrests for drug offences.

Members of the British royal family were rarely out of the limelight. In 1973 the marriage of Princess Anne to Captain Mark Phillips was broadcast to an estimated 100 million people worldwide. In 1970 she became president of Save the Children and was accompanied by journalists as she toured Africa extensively highlighting the charity's work. As a horsewoman, she also became news when she won the 1970 European Eventing Championship and competed in the British team at the 1976 Olympics.

◄ Manchester United and Northern Ireland footballer George Best at his Manchester boutique in 1970.

◄ The five finalists in the Miss World 1970 contest at the Royal Albert Hall: winner Jennifer Hosten (Miss Grenada), surrounded by (l-r) Miss Israel, Miss South Africa, Miss Africa South and Miss Sweden.

Other royals followed regularly by the press were Prince Charles and his latest girlfriend – newspapers were constantly speculating over whether he would marry – and Princess Margaret, sister of the Queen. As her marriage to Lord Snowdon failed, Princess Margaret was pictured stepping out with new partners.

The bedroom walls of teenage girls invariably featured giant posters of film, television and pop stars. Donny Osmond, David Cassidy and Michael Jackson, David Essex and the Bay City Rollers were all regularly depicted in pull-out double-page spreads from *Jackie*, the best-selling comic for young girls. Elton John became one of the most internationally known British pop stars at this time. His stage outfits were outrageous, even when glam rock was at its height.

At the Oscars, film fans cheered regularly for Jane Fonda, Diane Keaton, Jack Nicholson, Burt Reynolds, Robert Redford and Paul Newman.

▲ Elton John performs live at an open-air concert in Watford in May 1974.

As famous were pop stars such as Cher, and television star Farah Fawcett Majors (from *The Bionic Woman*). The turbulent romance of actors Richard Burton and Elizabeth Taylor meant that between 1974 and 1976 they divorced, remarried and divorced again, in the full glare of press photographers.

◄ Princess Anne and Captain Mark Phillips' wedding in 1973.

Politics

nstability and extremism were the hallmarks of politics in Britain during the 1970s. There were four General Elections, returning, on three occasions, Governments which could not achieve overall majorities.

The Labour Prime Minister, Harold Wilson, lost the first to Edward Heath in 1970. Wilson's defeat was a surprise but was largely attributed to the increasing popularity of Enoch Powell, a right-wing politician whose anti-immigration speeches were covered sympathetically in the popular press.

Edward Heath, the new Tory Prime Minister, introduced decimal currency and, in 1973, successfully negotiated Britain's membership of

the EEC (European Economic Community), the forerunner of the European Union. He also led a major reorganisation of Local Government in England and Wales.

Inflation and industrial unrest dogged Heath's time in office, leading to three-day working weeks to limit the use of electricity in response to miners' strikes in 1972 and 1974. Heath fought the General Election in February 1974 under the slogan 'Who Governs Britain?' – meaning the Government or the unions. The Conservatives won more votes but fewer seats than Labour.

◄ The Prime Minister, James Callaghan, and his wife Audrey at Brighton's Top Rank ballroom, prior to the opening of the 1977 Labour Party Conference.

▲ MPs Barbara Castle and Enoch Powell at the anti-Common Market national referendum campaign press conference at the Waldorf Hotel in London, 1975.

The far right National Front Party, forerunner of the British National Party, won increasing support with its call for forced repatriation of all 'non-white' immigrants.

Despite losing his Parliamentary majority in 1977, Callaghan held on to power with the backing of the Liberals under their new leader David Steele; this was known as the Lib-Lab pact. When the pact ended in 1978, Callaghan avoided a General Election and led a minority Government until 1979. By the time the election was called, Labour's popularity had dramatically declined. This was due mainly to industrial action by public sector workers in what came to be known as the Winter of Discontent.

Calls for devolution for Scotland and Wales gathered momentum. In 1974 almost a third of those voting in Scotland voted for the Scottish National Party and the party returned 11 MPs to Westminster. The Scotland Act of 1978 proposed a Scottish Assembly; in a referendum the following year, Scotland voted narrowly for the assembly but controversially did not achieve the required majority.

In Wales, support for Plaid Cymru increased throughout the decade, with three MPs taking their seats in Parliament after the 1974 election. However, Wales too rejected plans for an assembly in 1979 and support for Plaid Cymru declined.

In 1979 Margaret Thatcher became the Conservative party leader and won the 1979 General Election with a substantial majority of 44 seats.

However, Heath could not agree a coalition with the Liberals so Wilson became Prime Minister for a second term. He continued until 1976, resigning for health reasons, and the third Prime Minister in the decade, Jim Callaghan, took over.

As people searched for alternatives to Labour and Conservative, who were considered to be too similar, the Liberal Party enjoyed a surge of support under its charismatic leader Jeremy Thorpe at the 1974 General Election. The party's calls for political reform gathered widespread support, but its popularity declined when Thorpe was embroiled in a scandal.

War & Peace

The Cold War was the term to describe international tensions at the time. This referred to the relationship between the two superpowers and their allies, namely the USA and the Western European countries in NATO (North Atlantic Treaty Organization), and the Soviet Union and its allies in the Warsaw Pact.

The two sides avoided conflict in Europe by targeting massive arsenals of nuclear weapons at each other, in a policy suitably known as MAD (Mutually Assured Destruction). This meant that if one side fired nuclear weapons at the other, the other would immediately retaliate and the resulting global conflict would destroy the planet. The strategy meant that the two superpowers spent enormous amounts of money updating their nuclear weaponry in order to keep pace with the other and maintain the balance.

America and the Soviet Union also supported conventional international and civil wars in other parts of the world, most notably Vietnam. American forces backed the Government of South Vietnam fighting against the Government of North Vietnam, which was backed by the USSR. American involvement included sending troops to fight the war, while the Russians trained and supplied the North. US intervention provoked domestic and foreign protests, and in 1973 American forces pulled out of Vietnam.

▲ Cambodia under the Khmer Rouge: workers clear the grounds in front of an Angkor temple, 1978.

▲ The last-minute evacuation of authorised personnel and civilians from the US Embassy in Saigon, Vietnam, in April 1975.

The USA and the Soviet Union also supplied opposing forces in Central and South America, and in Africa. One of the most brutal struggles took place in Cambodia, where the Communist leader of the Khmer Rouge, Pol Pot, led a revolution against the US-backed Government; the result was millions of civilian deaths.

There were military coups during the decade, notably in Syria, when the Assad regime came to power, and in Ethiopia, where Haile Selassie was overthrown. In the Middle East, in 1973, the Yom Kippur war began when Egypt attacked Israel in order to recover territory it had lost in the 1967 war. When the United States backed

▲ An Indian soldier disarms Mukti Bahini irregulars at the edge of the Bihari minority quarter in Dacca, East Pakistan, December 1971.

Israel by supplying weapons, the Arab states announced an oil embargo against the USA and its allies, including the UK. The Arab states cut production and increased prices, contributing to the stock market crash which was a major factor in the ensuing world economic recession. After initial heavy losses, Israel successfully repulsed attacks from Egypt and Syria. The war concluded with a peace treaty signed in 1978 at Camp David, the country home of the US president.

There were bloody civil wars too, in Ethiopia, Argentina, and Chile, where the USA funded rebels to overthrow Salvador Allende, the leader of the world's first elected Marxist Government.

The country of Bangladesh was created following another conflict, involving India and West Pakistan on one side and East Pakistan on the other. Atrocities took place and millions of people became refugees. Pakistan suffered a humiliating defeat: at the end of the fighting, it

had lost more than half its population and nearly a third of its army was in captivity.

As the decade ended, the Russians invaded Afghanistan, and in Iran, the US-backed monarchy was ousted and replaced with a theocratic Islamist Government.

▲ Destruction from the bombing of Chbanieh, southern Syria, 1973.

In the News

Most people watched news bulletins on television, broadcast from national and local stations by the BBC and ITN. Local radio stations broadcast news from the BBC, and from October 1973 Independent Radio News provided new stations such as Capital with bulletins.

The economy and the effects of soaring inflation were daily topics as unemployment rose. Industrial disputes dominated the news with film of picket lines and studio interviews with trade union leaders, employers and Government ministers.

Coverage of industrial action was usually front-page news in the national press. Most newspapers were pro-Conservative, and so were highly critical of trade unions, campaigning against them and their leaders. The *Daily Mirror* was pro-Labour but, in a reflection of the turmoil that was engulfing the party at the time, it was far from wholehearted in its support for working people.

Most cities and towns had their own local and regional newspapers, but overall, sales were declining. Local newspaper ownership was

∧ A host of celebrities appear in a poster campaign launched by People for Europe, a non-party-political campaign to keep Britain in the EEC, 1975.

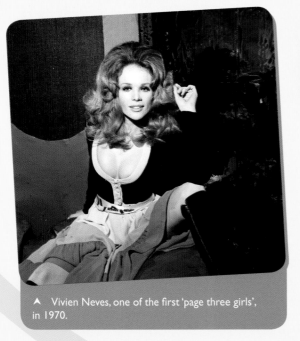

∧ Vivien Neves, one of the first 'page three girls', in 1970.

increasingly concentrated among a small group and much of the content was duplicated across editions serving different regions.

National newspaper sales too were declining. However, the most popular one, *The Sun*, increased its circulation significantly by featuring pictures of topless women. The success of 'page three girls' led other titles, such as *The Daily Star* and, for a while, the *Daily Mirror*, to do the same, despite protests and bans from public and university libraries.

In 1973 Britain became part of the European Economic Community (known as the 'Common Market'). The following year, the electorate voted

substantially in favour of membership with a 65 per cent turnout. The campaign for a 'Yes' vote was supported by Liberals and Conservatives, but Labour was neutral, allowing ministers to campaign for and against continuing membership. Every household received leaflets written by the 'Yes' and 'No' campaigns and by the Government. The most important issues, the Government leaflet said, were 'Food, Money and Jobs'. Broadcasts by the campaigners and news analysis programmes were extremely popular, attracting up to 20 million viewers at a time.

Crime and violence were regular issues, with bulletins showing graphic scenes of terrorism. In Northern Ireland, nationalist and unionist paramilitary groups attacked each other, soldiers and civilians, but the Provisional IRA took the fight to the British mainland, as this generated far greater publicity. They bombed pubs, coaches and national landmarks where soldiers and civilians were killed and injured. Days after IRA bombs in two Birmingham pubs killed 21 people and injured 182, the Government passed the Prevention of Terrorism Act to give itself wider powers. Six people were wrongly convicted of

▲ A banner is held aloft above black students in South Africa, in the township of Soweto, following the funeral of a 16-year-old black student who died in jail, 1976.

the bombings and spent 16 years in prison before their convictions were quashed.

News from abroad received far less coverage than events at home. International news stories throughout the decade regularly featured South Africa, whose apartheid Government was an international pariah. There was particular international outrage at reports of the 1977 Soweto uprising in which at least 176 people, most of them school students, died and over 1,000 were injured.

Sports

Two very contrasting summer Olympics were held in the 1970s: Munich in 1972 and Montreal in 1976. More than 7,000 athletes from 122 countries competed in the Munich Olympics, among them the American swimmer Mark Spitz, who won seven gold medals, and the Russian gymnast Olga Korbut. Britain won 18 medals, among them a gold for pentathlete Mary Peters. But the Games were overshadowed by an attack at the beginning of the event by eight Palestinian terrorists on the Israeli team, resulting in the deaths of 11 Israeli athletes and five of their attackers.

Four years later, at the Montreal Olympics in 1976, another gymnast, 14-year-old Nadia Comaneci was the star. It was also the first Olympics at which the USA's Ed Moses, who dominated men's hurdling for the next decade, won his first Olympic gold medal.

Despite increasing concern about football hooliganism in the domestic game, football retained its popularity. The England team went to the 1970 World Cup as champions but they were beaten

by West Germany in the quarter-finals and failed to qualify for the next tournament. It was a golden era for Scotland, however, with the team putting on its finest ever performance at the 1974 finals and appearing as the sole UK representative in 1978.

Television was influential in boosting some sports. With the arrival in many homes of colour televisions, the BBC made snooker a popular spectator sport with the new series *Pot Black*, in which leading snooker players competed in single-frame matches. Darts was another sport new to television, attracting millions of viewers, as did showjumping – one of the best-liked programmes at the time was the *Horse of the Year Show* from Wembley.

◀ Dennis Amiss smashes the ball during the England v India match in the cricket World Cup of 1975.

◄ USA's Ed Moses wins gold at the Montreal Olympic Games in 1976; he sets a new world record time for the 400m hurdles of 47.64 seconds.

▲ Royal Ascot in 1975.

◄ Anti-apartheid protesters outside Twickenham in the mile-long march to the ground where the Barbarians are playing South Africa, 1970.

The first cricket World Cup was held in England in 1975, in which the West Indies beat Australia in the final. The Formula One motor-racing season was covered in the new BBC programme *Grand Prix*, with Murray Walker and, from 1979, the former world champion James Hunt commentating.

Major sporting events played on Saturday afternoons were covered by the BBC's *Grandstand* and ITV's *World of Sport*. Both programmes comprised live coverage, news and summaries of the day's sport. Sports gambling centred mainly on football pools, greyhound racing (which was not televised) and horseracing. *World of Sport* introduced the 'ITV Seven', an accumulator bet linked to the races broadcast.

In apartheid South Africa, only white athletes could represent the country. As a result, in 1971 international sports federations agreed a boycott; they would not send sportspeople to play in the country and South African teams would not be welcome anywhere else. During the 1970s, however, some countries, especially Britain, Australia and New Zealand, tried to organise events against South African teams, particularly cricket and rugby union matches. These often provoked mass demonstrations. Matters came to a head in 1976, when 29 African nations refused to take part in the Olympics because of New Zealand's involvement in the Games – its rugby team was touring South Africa at the time.

Important Dates

1970

The Equal Pay Act means that for the first time, women and men must be paid the same wages for doing the same jobs.

1971

On 15 February Britain changes from £sd (pounds, shillings and pence) to decimal currency.

1972

An attack on the Israeli team at the Munich Olympics by Palestinian terrorists ends in the deaths of 11 Israelis, one German policeman and five terrorists.

1973

War in the Middle East is followed by an oil embargo, leading to economic collapse in the Western world.

1974

US president Richard Nixon resigns, thereby avoiding prosecution for his part in the Watergate break-in and bugging scandal.

1975

Genocide in Cambodia begins following the country's takeover by Pol Pot, the leader of the Khmer Rouge.

1976

The worst earthquake of the century leaves over 250,000 dead, destroying the Chinese city of Tangshan.

1977

Gay News is found guilty of blasphemous libel for publishing a poem about a homosexual centurion's love for Christ at the Crucifixion; this is the result of a private prosecution by campaigner Mary Whitehouse.

1978

In December, Spaniards vote in democratic elections, the first in Spain for nearly 40 years.

1979

Margaret Thatcher becomes the first female Prime Minister of Great Britain.

Acknowledgements

Written by Carol Harris. The author has asserted her moral rights.
Edited by Abbie Wood.
Designed by Jemma Cox.

All photographs have been supplied by PA Images.

Every effort has been made to contact the copyright holders; the publisher will be pleased to rectify any omissions in future editions.

Text © Pitkin Publishing.

Publication in this form © Pitkin Publishing 2014.

No part of this publication may be reproduced by any means without the permission of Pitkin Publishing and the copyright holders.

Printed in Great Britain.

ISBN 978-1-84165-541-3   1/14